IF THERE IS NO POWER

THERE IS NO PRAYER!

God ?

Are You Waiting To Hear From Me?

By Apostle G. Marie Carroll

No Power No Prayer

Unless otherwise noted all scripture is taken from the King James Version of the Bible.

If There Is No Power There Is No Prayer

Copyright© 2009 by Apostle G. Marie Carroll

ISBN: 1441465928
EAN: 9781441465924.

For more information contact (516) 833-5235 or visit:

www.myspace.com/apostlegmarie

kingdombuilders669@yahoo.com

Partial Editing Rickisha Hawkins

Printed in the United States of America.
All rights reserved under International Copyright Law. No part of this book may be reproduced or transmitted in any form or by any means, electronic or mechanical, including photocopying, recording, or by any information, storage and retrieval system, without the written permission of the author.

No Power No Prayer

I dedicate my second book to My Mother Prophetess Hattie Ruth Williams. My Mom is a strong and powerful prayer warrior.

Mom I remember when I was a child I stuck my hand in a wall socket and I was electrocuted. I recall my hand going limp, but I also remember that you prayed to God with such a fervent prayer that the blood began to flow in my hand again instantly. I know the power of prayer because you have demonstrated it time and time again.

You being the mother of 18 (13 living) 81 grandchildren and 30 great grandchildren have much experience in prayer. You have prayed away a multitude of fevers, viruses, rashes, headaches, financial woes and the list can continue to grow. I know that you have prayed for me on numerous occasions and I also know that your prayers are effective because God Hears You!

Mom, don't ever change even when you are misunderstood because someone is changing right in front of your eyes.

I Love You and I Bless God for You being who you are. Because of who you are I BECAME WHO I AM!! Keep on Praying It Works!!

Acknowledgements

MY husband Kenneth ,My son Charles(Salima), My daughter Rikki (Robert) My daughter Rickisha, My daughter Dionna, My grandchildren Nyisha, Quadrel, Charles III, Shaquan, Nejla, Robert Jr. I acknowledge all of you as Jewels in the Kingdom of God. I know that your lives will never be the same. It was because of Prayer that you all have the Power of a living God moving and shaking in your life for eternity. I Love you all.

To my Kingdom Family I love you all keep the faith and Pray, Pray, Pray!!

Contents

Introduction--------------------7

Chapter 1----------------------19

Chapter 2----------------------23

Chapter 3----------------------31

Chapter 4----------------------37

Chapter 5----------------------45

Chapter 6----------------------51

Chapter 7----------------------61

Chapter 8----------------------73

After word--------------------77

No Power No Prayer

Introduction

If there is no Power, There is no Prayer.

Prayer is really important if we have made plans to hear the voice of God. I have noticed that there is a spirit by the name of distraction whose main vocation is to shut off communication between God and His Children. In **Psalm 37:23** the bible lets us know that the steps of a good man are ordered by the Lord. But it is clear to me that if the good man cannot hear which steps to take that costly error could occur which could cause a shifting in this good man's destiny.

Jesus understood the importance of prayer and never allowed anything or anyone to come between Him and His communication with His Father. As disciples we also must follow Jesus Christ's example and make sure we are also putting our highest priority on prayer. We are told in the word of God to continue in prayer or to pray without ceasing. (1 Thess. 5:17)

If there is no power there is no prayer.

    I was a seamstress by trade and I recall the difficulty I experienced when I was getting married to my late husband in 1992. I was in the middle of sewing ten dresses and I was tired but an unusual exhaustion overcame me. This condition was to such an extent that I forgot to plug in my electric sewing machine. I remember trying everything to get the machine to operate but that machine would not come on. I immediately thought that it was broken and so I took out a needle and thread and began to finish sewing these 10 dresses by hand. It took me days upon days to hand sew those dresses. I can still remember toiling up until the very day of the wedding. I thought I was tired before, well now I was really tired.

This was a time that I really depended upon the Lord and He helped me through that one. I realized about a month later that the machine was never plugged into the outlet. When I tried the machine and it came on, the Lord told me what happened; He said "just as you did not plug in the machine, you were so busy that you were not plugged in to Me either. So I could not help you. I would have told you that the machine was unplugged if you had just once acknowledged me in your haste to finish your dresses".

The lesson I learned from this was tremendous. I took too long to finish the dresses and on top of it all I was really stressed out. This was a hard task and all because I never even thought to pray to the Lord about how to go about this project in the first place.

In this situation I was reminded that God wants His children to talk everything over with Him. I have learned that prayer is our personal conversation with our Father.

He is such a good Father and He just waits patiently while we do everything besides ask Him. His longsuffering nature allows us to go to our extremity and then our God takes the opportunity to be our Father and He lovingly comes to our rescue (if we ask Him) to put out the fires that we have started.

The power that we need is in our obedience. Father wants us to communicate with Him. He is right there, only a prayer away,

Isaiah 65:24 lets us all know that it shall come to pass when you call on him He will answer and while you are yet speaking He will hear.

No Power No Prayer

It is our responsibility to maintain a clear connection to our Father that we may hear His words.

At times I have experienced an unclear connection and I was even thinking "why is God not talking to me"? When I examined myself I found that it was me! I had placed cotton in my ears and I was not listening to God!

Let me tell you how it happened. One day I was praying and I heard the Lord give me instruction on how to get a CD recorded. Well I began the CD and when the going got tough and I started to face the adversary who came to stop me from what the Lord was saying I stopped dead in my tracks. After a few months of talking to God about what happened, I noticed that He stopped answering my petitions, I was thinking wow, you know the Lord must have taken a vacation or something because I am calling on Him and yet I cannot hear Him speaking.

When I inquired in the word of the Lord in **1John 1:9 I read If I confess my sins that God is faithful and just to forgive me of my sins and to cleanse me from all unrighteousness**. I began to think "well I have confessed my sins unto God", but I had left out something, the Lord made specific instruction for me to do the CD and I stopped. I was no longer using His word to speak to the mountains, no longer using God's word to slay the giants; I was just backing down forgetting all about the Greater One being inside of me.

God is so awesome and mighty and just that He will never, ever go back on His word. He said if we call upon Him He will answer, I called Him but I could not hear Him answer me because of my disobedience to His word.

No Power No Prayer

I found out that there is only one way and that way is obedience to the word of God. I tried to do it on my own and I found out the hard way. I realize that on my own I am powerless to do anything. God is absolute Power!!

In order to pray we must relinquish all fleshy ideas and allow ourselves to be open to the voice of God. In **Hebrews 11:6** the bible says that in order for us to please God we must first believe that He is... I have firsthand experience in this area as well.

I remember in my early Christian walk, I used to allow everyone else to pray over me, I was never taught to really connect in to God in prayer for myself. I have found in my travels throughout the Body of Christ that there are many who have not learned of their ability to speak with God for themselves.

No Power No Prayer

For many there is an ideology that our conversation with God is set aside for an elect few. This untruth has somehow fostered a belief in many that God has no time for an audience with them. I am here to remind you of the scriptures. Jesus told us in **Luke 11** that men must always pray and then He showed us the template for prayer. .

One night many years before I understood prayer I was at a Bible study and I was asked to pray for the meeting. I recall standing there feeling helpless and ashamed.

I remember thinking to myself, "Why are we talking to someone invisible, who probably either is not listening or does not exist anyway?" So my first experience was like, "Jesus? Uhm Uhm Please uhm....er.. Can you uhm help my family? I uhm.. thank you very much Amen."

No Power No Prayer

There was a thunderous applause when I finished and as I looked around sheepishly I vowed that these people would never get me in this situation again!! Well needless to say everywhere I went someone would ask me to pray and I would feel awkward but I would try and the "uhms" started forming into words and I started getting a steady flow and learned quickly how to ask God for something.

It took a little time for me to believe. I had no trouble believing who God is, but I had trouble believing that He could ever think I was somebody. In my travels among people I find this to be a major reason why most people have trouble communicating with God.

Most people think that they are so unworthy that God would never speak to them anyway so why even try to talk to Him. I know this because I used to be one of those people. I allowed others to make me feel condemned and I did not realize that there was a difference between condemnation and conviction. I had these two words confused and it hindered my walk with God. It would have been great to have the information that I now have. When I fell I could have gotten up and tried again, I could have asked God to forgive my sins and, I could have repented (turned away from sin) and tried again.

I know now that if I want my communication clear then I must stay connected to God. I cannot walk in disobedience and expect to hear the voice of God. I cannot walk in the flesh and expect my communication to be open. I cannot have a problem with my giving and expect a giving God to provide all my needs according to His riches in Glory.

I cannot expect Father to hear me if I don't know His Love

language. His Love Language is His Word. He does not speak flesh, He speaks Spirit, He does not speak death, He speaks Life, He does not speak fear, He speaks Faith, He does not speak cowardice, He speaks Courage, He does not speak failure, but our God speaks Victory.

If we really want a clear communication with God we must use the powerful word of God when we pray!

Hebrew 4:12 For the word of God is quick, and powerful, and sharper than any two edged sword, piercing even to the dividing asunder of soul and spirit, and of the joints and marrow, and is a discerner of the thoughts and intents of the heart.

God will honor His word. It is His Will, His Promise, His covenant, His Testament and our Inheritance. The Word is the Power of God. **Use It God Will hear YOU!**

No Power No Prayer

Back To Basics

John 1:1 "In the beginning was the word and the word was with God and the word was God."

Every answer that we need will be found in the beginning. In the book of Genesis we find the only powerful God framing worlds by speaking them into existence.

"Let there be light, a firmament in the heavens, the universe etc. Then let there be a man and I am going to form him from the dust of the ground and allow him to communicate with me.

I am going to give him superiority over the beasts of the field and over the fowl in the air, the fish in the sea and over anything that creeps on the ground, in other words I am giving Him dominion and power over everything on Earth!!

I will guide him, I will make him like me He will be just a little lower than the angels, The only thing I will need from him is obedience to my word and all that I own will be his"

Well needless to say this was not enough for Adam (the first Man) and Eve (the first woman) it seems that they still needed more. According to the Bible, God brought every animal in the Garden of Eden and instructed Adam to name them.

I believe it took conversation for this to happen. The Lord spoke to Adam and gave him commandments about everything including not to touch, taste or even look at the tree in the midst of the Garden, the tree of the knowledge of Good and Evil!

The Bible says in Genesis 3 that there was a serpent being used by satan and this serpent beguiled Eve by making her think that she and Adam would be as wise as God if they ate from this tree or that they would be gods. He told her to eat and she ate. She gave it to her husband also. They realized their nakedness and sewed fig leaves to cover their nakedness and even tried to hide from the presence of God behind the trees in the Garden.

Now according to some, who have not had an opportunity to hear the voice of God, God does not speak. Yet, here we have Him speaking to Adam and Eve in the Garden "where are you"? Adam told God he was naked and hiding! God then asked Adam how he knew about such a thing. Adam told God that the woman God gave him was to blame and then Eve told God that the serpent beguiled her and I can imagine the serpent telling God that satan tricked him and so it was a blame game.

To make a long story short their communication with God became damaged that very minute because of their disobedience and because of their unwillingness to accept the blame for what they had done. They were then given animal skins to cover their nakedness, and then they were expelled from the Garden of Eden. The two of them would never be permitted to return to the Garden of Eden lest they eat from the tree of life and be in a wicked, fallen state for eternity.

    The day that Adam and Eve ate in disobedience was the day that they could no longer hear God's voice. It was not because God stopped talking, it was because they were out of the position to hear.

Who Obeyed?

This is a list of some of the men and women of God who made a choice to listen to God's instruction

Genesis

- Abel gave a perfect sacrifice

- Noah built the ark according to all that the Lord said and saved his entire family from destruction.

- Abraham left his country and kinsmen as per the voice of the Lord and his obedience gave all the families of the world the ability to inherit his favor.

- Jacob held on to God until He blessed Him according to His word. Jacob's holding on allowed the

Twelve tribes to be birthed and out of the Twelve came the Tribe of Judah which was the Tribe Jesus Christ's lineage traced back to.

- Joseph one of Jacob's sons (Abrahams great-grandson) believed the dreams that he had. Because of his supernatural gifts his jealous brothers sold him into slavery He ended up in Egypt and went from the Pit (where his brothers kept him until they sold him) to the prison (After he refused the advances from Potiphar's wife) to the palace after interpreting the dreams of Pharoah. This was all because he obeyed the voice of the Lord which caused the Twelve tribes of Israel to escape famine and multiply in the land of Goshen under Joseph's rule.

Exodus
- Moses heard the word of the Lord through the burning bush and he led millions out of captivity from Egypt, through the wilderness and to the door of the promised land

Joshua
- Joshua heard the voice of the Lord and led the children of God out of the wilderness into the Promised Land. Tearing down walls to complete his mission.

Judges
- Deborah believed the word of the Lord and judged the nations.

- Barak believed the Lord and would not go to war without Deborah

1 Samuel

- Prophet (seer) Samuel obeyed the Lord and anointed King David even while there was a sitting King (disobedient Saul).
- God also used him to judge the house of the priest Eli because of the illicit acts of his sons. His sons caused the Ark of the Covenant to be stolen from the Tabernacle

Kings

- Prophet Elijah listened to the Lord and his obedience caused him to never taste death(translate

- Prophet Elisha obeyed the voice of the Lord and even his very bones in his grave had resurrecting power

Esther

- Esther saved a whole nation of Jews because she obeyed the word of God that her uncle Mordecai gave to her. Esther was not concerned about her self her concern was going in to see the King on behalf of her people.

Isaiah

- Prophet Isaiah obeyed the word of the Lord even though he was a man of unclean lips. He proclaimed that if the Lord needed somebody that he was available for service.

Daniel

- Daniel was used of the Lord to interpret dreams and visions for Kings. The spirit that was in him caused favor to follow him where ever he went. He was obedient to worship God and pray three times a day no matter what happened. His obedience to God caused favor to be upon him. The favor was so great that even when they put him in the Lions den he could not be devoured.

New Testament

- **Paul**

After Paul's conversion on the Damascus Road, he was an ardent supporter of Jesus Christ's ministry and knew that it was important to pray. Paul became one of the most powerful Apostles in history because of his ability to follow the principles of Jesus Christ to the letter. Once he met Jesus his whole life changed!

- **John The Baptist**

John the Baptist was obedient in his position as forerunner for the Messiah. He did not conflict with Jesus; he affirmed Jesus' authority by preaching the coming of the Kingdom.

Jesus

- Jesus the Christ, the anointed one and His anointing prevailed. Jesus above everyone in this list was able to obey every word that was given to him here on earth. We must remember that He is God wrapped in flesh who came here to set the captive free.

- He gave up his deity, and this was to show us that we can be obedient too. The bible says in Hebrews 5:8 Though He were a Son, yet learned He obedience by the things which He suffered; Jesus never failed to **PRAY!**

My Time To Pray

Prayer Defined- is the act of communicating with God in worship. Specific forms of this may include praise, requesting guidance or assistance, confessing sins, as an act of reparation or an expression of one's thoughts and emotions.

Personal prayer time must be implemented if one is to get personal with God. We must remember how Jesus always made time to be alone with God.

In Luke 11:1 "And it came to pass, that, as He was praying in a certain place, when He ceased, one of His disciples said unto Him, Lord, teach us to pray As John also taught his disciples."

No Power No Prayer

As followers of Jesus Christ we must be careful to do what He did if we want to have what He has.

In all situations Christ prayed first and then after hearing from God He would proceed to do what he was instructed to do.

Personal conversation with God was of utmost importance to Jesus. He would not utter a word without complete authority from God.

Jesus' relationship with God reminds me of the armed forces. No one makes a move without hearing from the President of The United States.

Somehow we are making moves without asking God if it is okay. We must have clearance from the one who can see our beginning and our end.

Rev 1:8 I am Alpha and Omega, the beginning and the ending, saith the Lord, which is, and

which was, and which is to come, the Almighty.

Keep it personal and just watch how the Lord will begin to minister to you about your personal life. Do not wait until Sunday to speak to the Lord about it. Do not wait until you come to church to lay it on the altar. Our modern day altar is our heart and our tongue should be repenting, confessing and believing.

Personal prayer is open communication with God. We must remember to wait right there for direction, wait right there for answers to our problems and listen for instruction. We must also remember to be a doer of the word and not hearers only

James 1:22-23 "But be ye doers of the word, and not hearers only, deceiving your own selves. For if any be a hearer of the word, and not a doer, he is like unto a man

beholding his natural face in a glass:"

If we find ourselves only listening to God speak but not implementing His word we will find that we are only fooling ourselves into thinking that we are doing something when all we are really doing is being religious.

We must remember that God is relational and rituals and lies have no place in His order of operations. It really is personal!

Prayer is as personal as snowflakes. Just like there are no identical snowflakes, there should be no identical personal prayers.

I have my own relationship with our Father and you should have your own relationship with our Father as well.

It is no different than our relationships with our natural

parents. My mother has 13 living children out of 18 and each of her children are different. There are no two alike; each one has a different personality, character, and even features that are different from one another. Our tastes in clothing, color schemes, talents and emotions, likes and dislikes are totally different from one another.

I will even venture to say that if the most basic things about us are so different then our personal relationship with our mother must be different as well.

When I speak to my mom we speak about Jesus and His love all day long. When she converses with my other siblings she may have a different conversation with them. It is a personal relationship.

John 14:13-14 "And whatsoever ye shall ask in my name, that will I do, that the Father may be glorified in the

Son. If ye shall ask any thing in my name, I will do it."

When we are speaking with our Father in heaven, we must understand that this is also personal; we must develop our own relationship with our Father. How do I speak to Him, how does He speak back to me?

How will I know that I have heard Him clearly? Is there a certain place that I should steal away to meet Him privately? These things will start to come clear when you have made up your mind that you want to be powerful. It is important to recognize that prayer is the most effective way to increase power! Remember it is personal.

A.S.K.
Accept Sovereign Kinship

Matthew 7:7-12 "Ask, and it shall be given you; seek, and ye shall find; knock, and it shall be opened unto you: For every one that asketh receiveth; and he that seeketh findeth; and to him that knocketh it shall be opened.

Or what man is there of you, whom if his son ask bread, will he give him a stone? Or if he ask a fish, will he give him a serpent? If ye then, being evil, know how to give good gifts unto your children, how much more shall your Father which is in heaven give good things to them that ask him?

Therefore all things whatsoever ye would that men should do to you, do ye even so to them: for this is the law and the prophets."

No Power No Prayer

There is a *command* that we ask God for what it is we need. Many have been looking at this as though it were just a nice little section in a good book, but this is a very powerful statement, which God really expects His children to implement.

How would we really feel if our earthly Fathers even thought that we had no faith in them to provide for us? How would our earthly fathers feel if we disrespected their ability to be our provider? How does God view our arrogance in trying to get things done without asking Him to guide us or us doing without because we were too proud to ask HIm for help? He has told us to ask and it shall be given, but our asking must be aligned with His word and we must be prepared to use that word when we pray. Jesus said ask, *asking is praying.*

1 John 5:14-15 "And this is the confidence that we have in Him, that, if we ask any thing according to His will, He heareth us: And if we know that He hear us, whatsoever we ask, we know that we have the petitions that we desired of Him."

In this passage of scripture we find the author John the disciple encouraging us to have confidence in Jesus Christ. He has already shown us in His word by multiple witnesses that what He says He shall perform in our time. Just ask! Our asking must be in the will of God. What are our promises in the word of God? This is what we shall pray unto God to perform for us. This asking must be accompanied by confidence and this confidence must be accompanied by belief and this belief must be accompanied by desire for the Lord to perform His word on our behalf.

No Power No Prayer

I often think about Jesus in His earthly ministry and how each time He glorified God that He would ask Him to show forth His own Glory to the people who were watching and waiting.

In **John 11** Jesus was informed that a dear friend of His by the name of Lazarus was very ill. Mary and Martha the sisters of Lazarus sent for Jesus to come and heal him. Jesus refused to go right away and told the disciples this sickness is not unto death but that God would be glorified and His Son would be glorified through the Father.

Jesus waited four days and then He came into Bethany to glorify God. If we really analyze this story we would find Jesus going against His fleshly desire to save His friend and choosing the will of God. God's will is that the greater good comes out of all that we pray for.

Jesus could have visited Bethany earlier and no one would have ever known that God is a resurrecting God and that He can do anything but fail. No one would have ever seen the Glory of God made manifest through His son Jesus Christ. God asked Jesus to do it this way and Jesus asked God to glorify Himself through Him.

We must remember that what we ask of God should be something that can glorify God through us. Our selfish desires or things that will just make man compliment us or applaud us are not necessary in this Kingdom Age. What is fundamental and more important is for us to ask the Lord His Will. **Thy Will Be Done On Earth as it is in Heaven**. Just ask the will of the Father in the Name of Jesus and it shall be given unto you.

John 15:7 Jesus says "if you abide in me and my words abide in you; you shall ask what you will and it shall be done unto you."

According to the word of God if we are to ask for anything

we must abide in Jesus Christ. God expects to hear the voice of His children in prayer but if we are not abiding in His son Jesus Christ, it will be impossible for us to hear God when He speaks.

Isaiah 65:24 "And it shall come to pass, that before they call, I will answer; and while they are yet speaking, I will hear."

This passage insures what I already know and that is before we can even ask our Father He already knows what we are going to say and the answer is already gone from His mouth. It is up to us to ask God His will.

There is so much power in asking the will of God. When we ask the will of God how can we miss getting each and every petition? He said He would never withhold any good thing from us.

No Power No Prayer

The Bible is full of inheritances that have not been collected by many in the body of Christ because we are not asking for what He has promised us. Many saints have gone to their graves and have never experienced the promise of an abundant life here on earth.

God is saying just ask, Jesus Christ came to remind us just ask, The Holy Ghost was given to walk with us and comfort us and to make intercession for us and is prompting us to ask for what is rightfully ours. **Just Ask!**

Philippians 4:19
But my God shall supply all your need according to his riches in glory by Christ Jesus.

No Power No Prayer

S.E.K.
Search Eternal Enduring *King*

Matthew 6:33 "But seek ye first the kingdom of God, and his righteousness; and all these things shall be added unto you."

What are you seeking first? What the Lord is really trying to get through to us is that there is value in seeking the Lord first. Seeking His righteousness and then watching how He will provide everything that we could ever want is a promise that can be fulfilled.

When I applied this scripture in a personal way I found something so deep about it. I found that what Jesus was seeking was the same thing that I should be seeking. I read about

No Power No Prayer

Jesus and I chose to dig deeper into the mystery of God and I found out that Jesus wanted the very thing for Himself that God wanted for Him and that is what made Him one with God, He put His desires aside, realizing that even His own life was of no value unless He followed the plan of God. What was He seeking? Like a treasure hunt He was after the will of God.

Jesus kept seeking; looking for God in every situation and then applying the principles that would bring forth the peaceable fruit of God. No matter what He aligned His life with the word of God. It was a perfect life, a righteous life and a God centered life. He found perfect peace and Joy because He followed Gods word.

Jesus came to seek those who were lost and when He found them he gave them kingdom keys and revelation to carry this word into the nations. He was seeking. It is up to us to seek the Lord now while He may be found, and it is clear that if we are not careful time will run out on us and we will not be able to seek or find God when we want Him!

Seeking the kingdom first has been such an issue with the body of Christ but the Lord is sending yet another word to get us to understand that nothing will change if we are not willing to change anything.

As long as we pray after we make moves and as long as we forget about the Lord until we find ourselves in a storm and as long as we continue to rob Him of tithes and offerings and as long as we leave Him home when we go to school, work or play and only pick Him up on an occasional Sunday or a special holiday or when we are sad or when we are happy we will find ourselves only getting part of the inheritance but not the fullness of joy as the Lord has promised us.

No Power No Prayer

Pray without ceasing is the commandment that we received from the Apostle Paul in his letter to the Ephesians:

Ephesians 6:18 "Praying always with all prayer and supplication in the Spirit, and watching thereunto with all perseverance and supplication for all saints;"

Seek to pray always and not just always but with all types of prayers and all types of supplications in the spirit. Personal prayer, intercessory prayer, corporate prayer, prophetic prayer and prayer in the spirit are necessary to perfect our prayer life. Seek to pray first and wait and see what the Lord will answer and then do what the Lord says to do no matter what anyone says.

I must make a comment here because I find in our search for God there will be some sent by the enemy to delay our destiny. This is the job of the adversary, to keep you from entering into the rest that is promised to those who seek God and His righteousness first. It is a treasure hunt and you must seek. In order to find you must seek Him first, if He is second or later He will not participate in the plan.

God is a jealous God and there shall be no other god before Him. Not your husband, nor your wife, nor your children, nor your home, your car, your money, your job or your hobbies can take the place of God. If we seek these things before Him He shall make them our god and we will become enslaved to the very thing that we have given priority to. Seek and you shall find.

Search the word to find Him. God will always be there. Psalm 24:1 lets us know that "**the Earth is the Lord's and the fullness thereof, the world and they that dwell therein.**"

This passage of scripture encourages us to know that it is not hard to find God if you are looking for Him, He really is everywhere. If you go to the highest heights He is there, if you go down to the deepest depths He is there, no matter where you are He is there. He knows our hearts, our desires, our needs, our thoughts. When we really seek God we will find that all that we were seeking Him for was inside of us all the time.

From the foundation of the world He already knew who we would be but it is up to us to come into being by making the right choices and allowing what is already inside of us to be stirred up. When we seek God we are really seeking to become all that He has already made us to be.

Everything we want is in seeking God, His desire for us is really our desire for ourselves but we are not tuned in to that reality as of yet. **Seek Him and allow the peace of God to surpass your own understanding.**

K.N.O.C.K.

Keep note of covenant Killers

There is an urgency that should be in our prayers that will infuse us with the power to pull down heaven. The Bible says God's will be done on earth as it is in heaven.

To get heaven on earth there will have to be portals that are opened where the angels can bring the very fragrance of Heaven into our realm.

I often think about Christ's ministry on earth and I find Him to be one of the most persistent personalities that I have ever encountered. Christ would not let anyone or anything keep Him from the presence of the Lord. Christ would not allow anything to cause Him to be disobedient in the assignment that God sent Him to complete.

No Power No Prayer

In Matthew the 4th chapter, we find the spirit leading Jesus up into the wilderness to be tempted by the devil and there were 3 temptations that he suffered. These temptations were examinations of his pride, lust of the eyes and lust of the flesh. These three are the downfall of many men and many women.

Jesus prepared Himself for major tests of strength by overcoming this temptation with the word of God. We must recognize how powerful words are but be aware of how supernaturally powerful God's words are.

The bible says if you decree a thing it shall be established, which means our words can cause heaven to shake and loose those things we have been knocking for.

Father has already told us to place a demand, remind Him of His word and watch Him move.

No Power No Prayer

There is a parable in the Bible that speaks about a friend coming over to borrow some bread for his family and he knows that the man of the house is at home. Well he begins to knock and there is no answer and then he knocks a little bit harder and there is no answer and then he persistently knocks until there is an answer. The Lord wants us to be persistent with our knocking.

Don't give up after you have knocked the first time. He doesn't want us to be impatient about our knocking but knock with a surety that you will get an answer. Knock like you know someone is there behind the door.

No Power No Prayer

When we are expecting an answer from our Father we must make sure that our lives are in alignment with God's word. He cannot hear any knocks that are made with an unrighteous fist.

It is so important that we as children of God understand the principles of God. He is looking for us to be sin free, holy and acceptable unto him. He expects us to come to Him reverently and with the understanding that He is a just and righteous Judge and He would never lie to us.

If we are waiting in expectancy for our Father to answer our knock then we will be in the position for Him to shower us with His blessing.

Many times we look for God to honor His word, yet we are knocking on the door of blessings with a dirty fist. He loves us too much to visit us while we are in sin.

No Power No Prayer

The most powerful tool that Christians should be thankful for is forgiveness. Father is seeking those who will search their hearts and if they find anything that is not like Him, ask God's forgiveness and be sure that you are not holding anyone else hostage because you are not forgiving.

Father wants to talk to us but He cannot speak to us according to His own moral code unless we abide by the basic instructions His word, the Bible.

The Bible says God is a consuming fire to the wicked, but a refiner's fire to the righteous. Jesus says knock, He is planning to open everything unto us. Be persistent don't just accept whatever anyone wants you to have.

Knock to be delivered, knock to be set free, knock to cancel illnesses, knock to learn the word, knock to save your family, knock to save your marriage, knock to start your ministry, knock to get into the presence of the Lord, knock to get a new job and knock to pray effectively.

Knocking to get God's attention is similar to pressing. Pressing is never giving up; knocking is like staging a sit in.

Jacob knocked when he wrestled with the Angel of God all night long because he needed something from God that he could get from no other. He told the angel of God I will not let you go until you bless me. He was really knocking.

Knocking can be compared to radical praise, and no matter what the situation looks like we are still praising our God. It could be gloomy outside but we are still knocking until the Son opens the door.

When we understand how the Lord has a certain way in which He does His universal business which is already ordered, we will be in a position to reap the rewards of the Bible.

I often say in my lessons that I want the words of my Bible to jump off the pages into my life and I realize the only way that this will happen is if I knock as hard as I can. I must expect an answer!

When things look gray, I will knock with the scripture; **Nehemiah 8:10 " the joy of the Lord is my strength"** and when I feel fear, I will knock with the scripture **2Timothy 1:7 "for God has not given us the spirit of fear but of power and of Love and of a sound mind"** and if I find myself in a situation where a loved one has passed away I must knock with the scripture **2Corinthians 5:1 "for we know that if this earthly house of this tabernacle were dissolved there is a building of God not made by hand eternal in the heavens"** and when my faith seem to waver I knock with the scripture **2Corinthians 5:7 "for**

we walk by faith and not by sight" and when I am being persecuted I knock with the scripture **Isaiah 54:17 "no weapon formed against me shall prosper and every tongue that shall rise against me in judgment I shall condemn, this is the heritage of the servants of the Lord and God has said my righteousness is of Him."**

Each child of God has a responsibility to know the full will and testament in order to lay claim to the inheritance.

Knock and keep on knocking. When we knock it lets God know that we trust that He is on the other side of the door and that He will answer us because we are His children. When we knock with God's word we let Him know that we put our total trust in Him and that we are not trying to be self sufficient but we are God sufficient and that He has more than enough with Him. Just knock and He will answer and open the eyes of your understanding.

Knocking releases our power and when we have power it is the ultimate proof that we have been praying. **When there is no power, there is no prayer.**

No Power No Prayer

Pray For Power

Matthew 6:9-13

⁹**After this manner therefore pray ye: Our Father which art in heaven, Hallowed be thy name.**

¹⁰**Thy kingdom come, Thy will be done in earth, as it is in heaven.**

¹¹**Give us this day our daily bread.**

¹²**And forgive us our debts, as we forgive our debtors.**

¹³**And lead us not into temptation, but deliver us from evil: For thine is the kingdom, and the power, and the glory, for ever. Amen.**

In **Matthew 6: 9-13** we find Jesus giving us a template for prayer but we must recognize that templates are not to be repeated they are to be modeled. Effectual prayer causes power to manifest in our lives.

James 5:16 Confess your faults one to another, and pray one for another, that ye may be healed. The effectual fervent prayer of a righteous man availeth much.

When we examine this scripture we must take note that effectual means—powerful and fervent means persistent, hot boiling, something that has caused us to move from believing to knowing that we know and nothing can shake our belief.

What is really significant about this verse is the word righteous. In order to get God to answer we must be righteous. Righteous mean upright, it means holy, it means sold out to God and His will for our lives.

Father keeps showing me the waterfall with everything we

would need pouring out of His spirit. All we have to do to be sopping wet with His Glory is to follow His direction by the letter.

The Bible says we must listen; line by line, precept upon precept here a little there a little (Is 28:13)

When we are out of position we are powerless to move in the full authority of God. We want to see His miracles, signs and wonders, we want to be able to cast out devils, we want to be able to heal the sick and raise the dead, we want to be able to set the captive free and deliver everyone that comes in contact with us. Jesus never failed to get results from the Father because He never failed to consult with God about everything.

When we remember His word and reflect back on the feeding of the five thousand we find that Jesus prayed over two fish and five barley loaves of bread that ultimately fed 5,000 people and still 12 baskets were left over. I studied this scripture and the Lord revealed to me that Jesus had a serious key that He was trying to give to us. When we are trying to get God's attention we must come to him broken and contrite just like the bread which was broken to feed the five thousand.

We must come acknowledging that whatever He decides is alright because we are after the will of God for our lives.

We must trust God totally if we are to reign with power and authority in the end times. I must stress that prayer is the power tool for those who want to see the greater work that Christ mentioned in **John 14:12** manifested.

Verily, verily, I say unto you, He that believeth on me, the works that I do shall he do also; and greater works than these shall he do; because I go unto my Father.

Our Father which art in Heaven

This is an acknowledgement of God and where He is you may repeat this if you like but all things are asked in Jesus' Name so try

Father In The Name of Jesus

Hallowed be thy name

Is an adoration, letting God know that His name is Holy in all the earth.

I use this opportunity to say:

You are wonderful and magnificent and powerful and omniscient and omnipotent and omnipresent and I Love you and adore you. I give you all the Glory and the Honor for you are everything to me. You are my Savior, my King and my Lord.

Thy Kingdom Come

I don't say this part because I recognize that His kingdom came when Christ released the kingdom to us with his life, death, resurrection and ascension. The day the Holy Spirit came to the church and filled each and every believer with power from on high was the day that the Kingdom of God came inside of us.

Thy will be done,

Whatever you want to do in my life Lord do it, not my will but yours Father. I live to Worship You so no matter what, I want you to rule and reign in my life forever

On earth as it is in heaven

Father I recognize that you gave me keys to place a demand on heaven to come to earth. You said in your word in **Matthew 16:19 that whatsoever we bind on earth shall be bound in heaven and whatsoever we loose on earth shall be loosed in heaven. I decree that your Glory will fill the earth and all will come to know you for themselves.**

Give us this day our daily Bread

Thank you Father for the provisions for this day, I thank you that you were true to your word when your servant David stated never has he seen the righteous forsaken nor his seed begging bread. I thank you that you have always taken care of my family and me.

And forgive us our trespasses

*Forgive me of my sins Father In **1John 1:9 your word states that if we just confess our sins unto you that you are just and faithful to forgive us of our sins and to cleanse us of all unrighteousness** and we want to be clean Father that we may inherit everything that is promised. Forgive me for sins of omission and commission, my thoughts, my words, my deeds. Father I want to live holy before you. Please help me to do it like **you** want it done.*

As we forgive those that trespass against us

Father I forgive all that have trespassed against me and I ask you to forgive me for holding on to un-forgiveness .I release everyone now (usually I name names) Father please give me a heart like yours which is over flowing with unconditional Love!

And lead us not into temptation

Father in 2 Corinthians 10:4, 5 your word states: For the weapons of our warfare are not carnal, but mighty through God to the pulling down of strong holds ;)

Casting down imaginations, and every high thing that exalteth itself against the knowledge of God, and bringing into captivity every thought to the obedience of Christ;

So Father keep my mind, help me to cast down imaginations and every high thing that exalts itself against your knowledge, help me to capture every foul thought and bring it under the obedience of Christ Jesus. Help me to live holy and righteous that I may be a witness to those who are watching my life.

But deliver us from evil

*Father your word states there is no temptation known unto man that you will not give us a way of escape. In your word you said if we submit our lives unto you we will be able to resist the devil and he will flee from us. I submit Father, my way, my life, my will I **submit** unto you. Make me mold me after your likeness and to the stature of your son Jesus Christ.*

For thine is the Kingdom and the Power and the Glory Forever Amen

*In Psalm 24:1 Father **you let us all know that the Earth is yours and the fullness thereof, the world and they that dwell therein.** This is your Kingdom this is your power and all the Glory belongs to you. Father I Love you and I need you for there is no one else like you. It's Your Power, Your dominion, Your Glory and Your Authority.*

All these blessings in the name of the Lord Jesus Christ.

Amen (And it is so) It is sealed.

  This is how the Lord uses me to pray in a personal way and sometimes it depends on what the Lord wants, my prayers are subject to change. Do not forget Prayer is personal and it is how personal your relationship is with God.

The Holy Spirit will lead you and Guide you. Who would know what the Lord wants to hear better than the creative part of God. He will help you to create the perfect prayer, a prayer that will go directly into the throne room to be intercepted by Christ the one who will petition God on your behalf.

This power that we have been given is so that we can enter boldly unto the throne of grace and know that if we do it God's way we will never have our prayers go unanswered.

We would truly experience that prophetic word out of **Isaiah 65:24 where the Lord said and it shall come to pass that when you call I will answer and while you are yet speaking I will hear.** *We want the power that prayer brings into our lives.*

No Power No Prayer

Intercessory Prayer

Intercessory prayer is a prayer that is not personal and is not about you! Intercessory prayers are prayers that cause the prayer to stand in the gap for others. Many intercessors pray for the government because when the government is righteous the people live in peace and prosperity but when the government is corrupt there is turmoil in the land. An intercessor does not judge the government they just pray that the Lord makes right those things that are out of order and clean and purify those in authority.

Intercessors pray for nations, leaders and ministries as well as families of the world. Corporations, congregations, services, prosperity, healing, souls that come in from the rain and anything and anyone except themselves.

This is a God centered prayer and it is truly a ministry that the Lord uses to Glorify Himself here on earth.

In Romans 8: Likewise the Spirit also helpeth our infirmities: for we know not what we should pray for as we ought: but the Spirit itself maketh intercession for us with groanings which cannot be uttered.

And he that searcheth the hearts knoweth what is the mind of the Spirit, because he maketh intercession for the saints according to the will of God.

The Holy Spirit is the great Intercessor. Holy Spirit intercedes for us in prayer to Jesus Christ who then intercedes for us with the Father.

Holy Spirit will use a language that we cannot understand to convey to God what is really in our hearts There may be times we are too weary to pray but our Spirits will know what to pray for.

Intercessory prayer is a useful tool for church empowerment. Many principalities and strongholds are destroyed because the intercessor has a strong relationship with God. This relationship causes gifts to be made manifest. The gift of discerning of spirits (1 **Cor. 12**) is often given by the Holy Spirit to those with an intercessory prayer mantle.

For Power one must pray without ceasing **Ephesians 6:18 Praying always with all prayer and supplication in the Spirit, and watching thereunto with all perseverance and supplication for all saints;**

Praying for someone other than your self will yield the peaceable fruit of God. While you wage a good warfare to help someone else the Lord will fight your battle. You can be sure that He will be on your side no matter what may come your way **Power Up!**

Jesus Saves

In the Book of Romans 10:9,10 it states,

that if you confess with your mouth the Lord Jesus and believe in your heart that God has raised Him from the dead, you will be saved. [10] For with the heart one believes unto righteousness, and with the mouth confession is made unto salvation.

Father I confess with my mouth the Lord Jesus and I believe in my heart that your son Jesus Christ died for my sins and is now sitting on your right hand. I make Him Lord over my life and I am saved!1

If you have said these simple words, please find yourself a bible based church and plant your self there and Grow

After word

I pray that this book has encouraged your heart to pray more.

I have found that there is a force that wants you to feel silly about praying to God. Don't listen, just pray anyway!

God wants to hear our every word.

I often tell my congregation here in NY that God just wants to know that we know that He knows what is really going on in our day to day lives.

He is concerned about us and He wants us to live in victory every waking hour of our lives. Our prayers can be as simple as a parking spot in the mall; He wants to direct you to the nearest spot. When you get it don't forget to acknowledge that He had the foresight to make this happen.

He wants us to be happy, comfortable and confident as we walk this narrow way toward Him.

In all seriousness God said in His word in **Amos 3:7 "Surely the Lord GOD will do nothing, but He revealeth His secret unto His servants the prophets."**

I believe this scripture with my whole heart and I know it to be the truth. If we are truly listening to God we will never be surprised because He will reveal His plan to us.

Remember, it is our belief in what He says that will keep us in perfect peace.

In **Jeremiah 29:11** God gives Jeremiah a prophetic word
"For I know the thoughts that I think toward you, saith the LORD, thoughts of peace, and not of evil, to give you an expected end."

No Power No Prayer

Our Alpha and Our Omega Knows everything, we really need to just **TRUST HIM!**

Proverbs 3:5, Trust in the LORD with all thine heart; and lean not unto thine own understanding.

In all thy ways acknowledge him, and he shall direct thy paths.

I remember riding along the highway with my husband and all of a sudden the tractor trailers were moving into the left lane. I made my husband aware (he was driving) and he moved with them.

As we moved further down the road we saw a policeman directing the cars to the left and to the right and just as our vehicle went through traffic was stopped and all the cars behind us were stopped because of a major accident.

The Lord began to reveal Himself to me. He said "did you

recognize what happened?" Yes. He said "look at the tractor trailer." He said" you see how high he sits up above your car?" Yes Lord. "I can be compared to a tractor trailer. I can see much further than you, I can see everything that will try to come against you; I can see the good and the bad. **Just FOLLOW ME!"**

FOR MAXIMUM POWER STAY CONNECTED **IN PRAYER!**

WHERE THERE IS NO POWER THERE   REALLY IS NO PRAYER!

Grace and Peace,
Apostle G. Marie Carroll

About The Author

Apostle G. Marie Carroll

Chief Prelate of Kingdom Builders

International Movement For Christ Inc.

Renowned recording artist, Vocalist, Writer, Producer, Minister of Music, pianist, Playwright, Poet, Author, Radio/Television personality, actress clothing/clergy Robe designer

Gwendolyn Marie Middleton was born to the late Joseph Middleton and Prophetess Hattie Ruth Williams on April 13, 1952. Apostle G. Marie was called to form Kingdom Builders International Ministries for Christ Church, Inc. on April 13, 2002 and was installed as Pastor on April 10, 2004.

Apostle G. Marie has ministered in many churches along the Eastern seaboard and has now been offered

No Power No Prayer

ministry opportunities in Europe and Africa. Apostle G. Marie is a wonderful vessel sent by God for such a time as this. She is highly recognized in the body of Christ as an end time Prophet that reveals current truth with boldness. Her main goal is to empower the children of God to embrace The Kingdom Principles as outlined in Ephesians the fourth chapter. She is dedicated to teaching the body of Christ to mature to the fullness of Christ that we all may comprehend His purpose for our lives.

She is the wife of Bishop Kenneth Carroll- Pastor of Kingdom Builders Int'l, Mother of Pastor/Prophet Charles Jenkins, Jr.(Salima), Mother of Prophetess Rikki Fuller (Min. Robert Fuller), Mother of Prophetess/Teacher Rickisha Hawkins, and Mother of

No Power No Prayer

Interpreter Dionna Smith. Grandmother to Evangelist Nyisha, Prophet Quadrel, Minister Charles Jenkins III, Minister Shaquan Fuller, Apostle Nejla Nicole-Rae Jenkins, Prophet Robert Lamarr Fuller, Jr.. She is also the spiritual mother to many who hold her ministry in the body of Christ in high esteem.

Apostle G. Marie was affirmed to the sent office of Apostle and Chief Prelate on April 8, 2006 with a host of Apostles, Prophets, Evangelists, Pastors, Teachers, Bishops, Elders and ministers. She vows to continue to lead the lost to the Cross and hopes and prays that many are saved by the work God is doing through her life.

Ministry Tools by Apostle G. Marie Carroll

Books

Power of the Five-Fold For the perfecting of the Saints...

If There Is No Power There Is No Prayer

Work Books-

To be used in conjunction with our Low cost seminars

Close your eyes and pay your tithes- A comprehensive teaching on tithes and offerings

Prayer 101- learn how to pray when you are home alone

Yes Lord I hear You- a complete study on How to hear the Voice of God

No Power No Prayer

Word Tapes

I have my mind on my covenant

Crackers and Juice

It's all Good

The power is in me

Don't walk Run

First things First Obey Your Thirst

Go For What God Knows

My Trust is a Must

God Loves You and He's using

me to let you know

For more info write:

kingdombuilders669@yahoo.com

Music CD's

Inspirational Blessings

I Can't Forget Jesus Changed Me

I am the God that healeth thee,

Healing Soaker CD with

Scriptures read by Prophet Mike

Wills and vocals by Apostle G.

Marie Carroll

DVDS

Apostle G. Marie in Concert 2006

Apostle G. Marie at Westbury Music Fair 2007

Apostle G Marie at AICC for Christmas Joy 2007

Apostle G. Marie in Brooklyn Helping the Haitian Mission to fund raise 2008

Helen Baylor and Apostle G. Marie at Brownsville for Jesus Festival 2008

Another Time At The Kingdom (Television Show)

Poems

The Last will and Testament of
the Most High God

When I praise Him

Time

The Ark

Stay In Your Lane

Women Of Grace Walking By
Faith

And many More

Plays

Adam and Eve

Cain and Abel

The five foolish and the five wise

The Closer I Get to you the
further I am from Him!

Thank You for your support. If
you need more information on
our ministry materials, please

email us at

kingdombuilders669@yahoo.com

and we will E-mail our ministry

brochure to you.

www.myspace.com/apostlegmarie

Kingdom Builders 610-612

Woodfield Road

West Hempstead NY 11552

(516) 833-5235

Made in the USA